SWIMMING

FOR FUN!

By Andrew Willett

Content Adviser: Conrad Johnson, Senior Manager/Masters Swimming Team, YWCA, New York, New York
Reading Adviser: Frances J. Bonacci, Reading Specialist, Cambridge, Massachusetts

COMPASS POINT BOOKS

MINNEAPOLIS, MINNESOTA

Compass Point Books
3109 West 50th Street, #115
Minneapolis, MN 55410

Visit Compass Point Books on the Internet at *www.compasspointbooks.com*
or e-mail your request to *custserv@compasspointbooks.com*

Photographs ©: Zac Macaulay/Getty Images, front cover (left); Artville, front cover (right), 5; Corel, 4–5, 28–29, 42 (left & right), 43 (left), 44, 45 (bottom); Donald Miralle/Getty Images, 7; Harry How/Getty Images, 8–9; Courtesy of Spirit Aquatics, 10 (left), 11; PhotoDisc, 10 (right), 12–13, 29, 30–31; Indiana University, 13; Al Bello/Getty Images, 15, 32–33, 43 (right); Adam Pretty/Getty Images, 23, 24–25; Mike Powell/Getty Images, 27; Donald Miralle/Getty Images, 35; IOC Olympic Museum/Getty Images, 37; Gary NBewkirk/Getty Images, 40; Tony Duffy/Getty Images, 41; Getty Images Hulton Deutsch/Getty Images, 45; Robert Cianflone/Getty Images, 16–17; Jeff Gross/Getty Images, 18–19; Darren England/Getty Images, 20–21; Nick Wilson/Getty Images, 38–39.

Editors: Ryan Blitstein/Bill SMITH STUDIO and Catherine Neitge
Photo Researchers: Christie Silver and Sandra Will/Bill SMITH STUDIO
Designer: Jay Jaffe/Bill SMITH STUDIO

Library of Congress Cataloging-in-Publication Data
Willett, Andy (Andrew)
    Swimming for fun! / by Andy Willett.
      p. cm. — (Sports for fun)
    Summary: Describes the four racing strokes in the sport of swimming and
    presents information on the basic equipment, practice, coaching, and competition.
    Includes bibliographical references and index.
    ISBN 0-7565-0432-5 (hardcover)
    ISBN 0-7565-1162-3 (paperback)
    1. Swimming—Juvenile literature. [1. Swimming.] I. Title. II. Series.
    GV837.6.W53 2003
    797.2'1—dc21   2002014597

Table of Contents

Ground Rules

Strokes, Starts, and Turns

People, Places, and Fun

Note: In this book, there are two kinds of vocabulary words. Swimming Words to Know are words specific to swimming. They are in **bold** and are defined on page 46. Other Words to Know are helpful words that aren't related only to swimming. They are in ***bold and italicized***. These are defined on page 47.

Get in the Water!

Do you know how to swim? You should. Everybody should know how to swim. It's a skill that saves lives. There's more to swimming than keeping your head above water. For thousands of years, people have trained to swim as fast as they can.

All around the world, men, women, boys, and girls work out with swim teams. Some of them train because they love to win races. Some of them train because they want to be in shape. All of them train because they love to swim.

The world of swimming is tons of fun. Jump on in. The water's great!

In the Pool

Olympic swimming pools are fifty meters [one hundred sixty-four feet] long and twenty-five meters [eighty-two feet] wide. They are at least two meters [seven feet] deep. Long cables called **lane lines** separate the pool into ten lanes.

The pool is marked so swimmers know where they are. Heavy, black **bottom lines** are in each lane. There are also **targets** at each end. They help swimmers move in a straight line. Each bottom line ends in a **T** two meters from the wall. When swimmers see them, they know to turn around. Backstroke swimmers need warnings, too. **Backstroke flags** are hung above the water, five meters [sixteen feet] from each end.

Swimmers go fastest in deep, still water. Pools are made to keep waves from forming. The lane lines *dampen turbulence*. The pool is also surrounded by **gutters** that help lessen waves. Look at the picture to learn the names of the parts of the swimming pool.

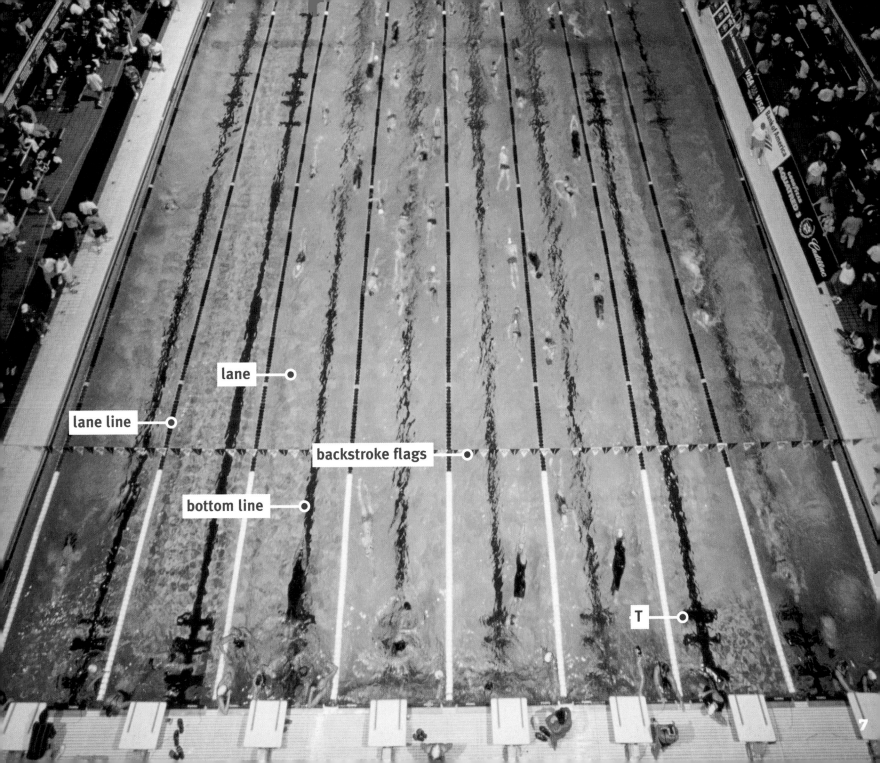

lane

lane line

backstroke flags

bottom line

T

How Long?

Swim meets are held in four kinds of swimming pools. The pools can be measured in either meters or yards. A **long-course** pool measures fifty meters or fifty yards long. A **short-course** pool is twenty-five meters or twenty-five yards long.

What difference does this make? A meter is a little more than a yard. So a 100-meter race is a little bit longer than a 100-yard race. Also, a 100-meter race in a short-course pool has three turns in it. The same race in a long-course pool has only one turn. Those differences may seem small, but to swimmers they seem huge. Turns can actually speed swimmers up and cause faster times!

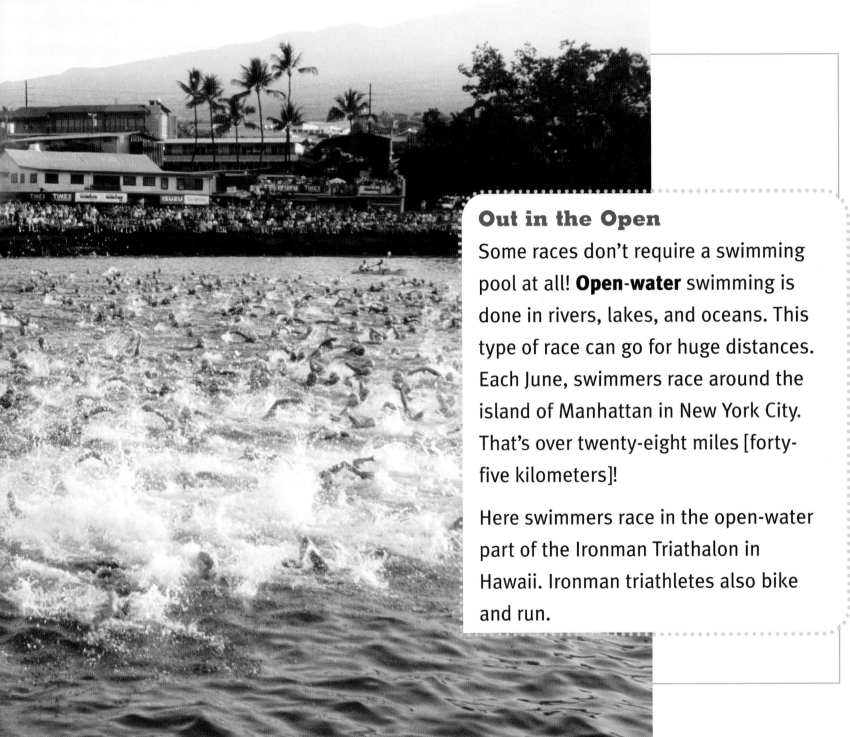

Out in the Open

Some races don't require a swimming pool at all! **Open-water** swimming is done in rivers, lakes, and oceans. This type of race can go for huge distances. Each June, swimmers race around the island of Manhattan in New York City. That's over twenty-eight miles [forty-five kilometers]!

Here swimmers race in the open-water part of the Ironman Triathalon in Hawaii. Ironman triathletes also bike and run.

Suiting Up

All swimmers wear swimsuits. They reduce **drag**, which is the water pushing against a swimmer. Drag slows swimmers down. Loose clothes create drag, so swimsuits fit tight against the body. Some swimmers now race in full-body suits. These special suits cut drag down even more.

Goggles let swimmers see clearly under water. They also protect the eyes from chemicals in the pool. Every face is different, so be sure to try on several different kinds of goggles before buying a pair. They should fit comfortably on the swimmer's face without leaking.

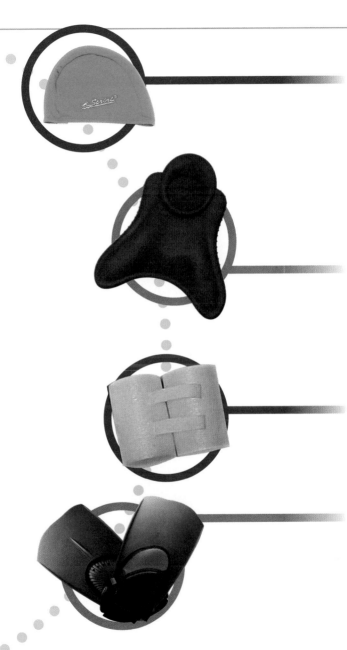

A cap keeps hair out of a swimmer's eyes. It also protects hair from chemicals.

Swimmers use different tools to make themselves stronger. They also help practice good technique.

Kickboards strengthen the lower body. Swimmers hold the board in their hands while using their legs to move across the pool.

Pull buoys are held between the thighs. This helps swimmers use only their arms to swim across the pool.

Fins for the feet and paddles for the hands make swimmers work harder to move through the water. They also make swimmers move very fast!

Show Me How

One thing every swimmer needs is a good coach. A coach is experienced in swimming and teaching others how to swim.

This book teaches you the basics. However, books can't watch you swim, and they don't know your name. Coaches spend time working with swimmers on the basics and *strategies*. They help swimmers to correct parts of their strokes. These mistakes could cause *injuries* or slow them down. Good coaches also get swimmers excited. They make them want to keep swimming even when they're tired.

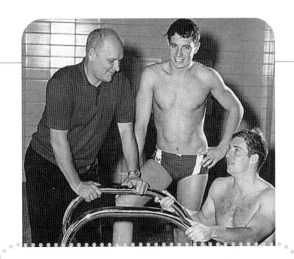

The Swim Doc

Dr. James "Doc" Counsilman coached Indiana University's swim team from 1959 to 1990. He also coached the U.S. Olympic Team twice. During his career, Counsilman's teams won twenty consecutive Big Ten championships and twenty-one Olympic gold medals. In 1979, he became the oldest man to swim the English Channel, at the age of fifty-eight.

Swim Free

A stroke is a way to move the legs and arms to swim. Swimmers learn four strokes: **freestyle**, **backstroke**, **breaststroke**, and **butterfly**. Freestyle is the fastest stroke. It is also the easiest to learn.

Swimmers stretch their body across the surface of the water. They look ahead so that their hairline is even with the surface. Freestyle swimming uses a **flutter kick**. Swimmers kick with one leg, then the other. They point their toes and relax their ankles. The legs should stay pretty straight. This kick gets power from the muscles of the buttocks and thighs.

Arms pull swimmers through the water. One hand goes into the water in front of them. The other pushes the water past their thighs. The shoulders roll from side to side. The head stays still. Most swimmers take a breath every two or three strokes. Swimmers breath by rolling their body and face toward the surface.

Ride High

No matter what stroke they are doing, swimmers always try to keep their body near the surface. The body moves faster through air than through water.

On Your Back

Backstroke is a lot like freestyle. Swimmers are on their back instead of their stomach. Because the face is always out of the water, it's easier to breathe. There's only one problem with this stroke. Swimmers can't see where they are going! They have to watch for backstroke flags to warn that they're close to the wall.

Backstroke uses a flutter kick. A swimmer's hands pop out of the water down by the thighs. They chop into the water up over the head. Swimmers scoop the water above their head down to their shoulder. Then they push the water down to their hips. Their shoulders roll from side to side, just like in freestyle.

Swim, Don't Sink!

Try not to "sit down" in the water when swimming backstroke. Tilting the head back helps a lot. If swimmers are indoors, they should look at the ceiling above them during the backstroke.

Practice, Practice

Drills are exercises that help a swimmer practice. Here are some freestyle and backstroke drills:

6 / 6 Rotation: This helps practice side-to-side **rotation** and kicking. Swimmers start on their side. The "low" hand is in front. The "high" hand is at the side. They kick six times, then take a stroke. They roll all the way over, and take six kicks on the other side. For freestyle, they roll across their front. For backstroke, they roll across their back.

Fingertip Drag: In freestyle, keeping the elbows high helps a swimmer rotate the right way. Swimmers drag their fingertips across the surface of the water. This helps keep the elbows up.

Pour Me a Cup

Swimmers should tip their head back during the backstroke. If they do, their hips will be in the right place. The hips should be up at the water's surface. To practice this, balance a plastic cup on the forehead while swimming.

Pull, Kick, Glide

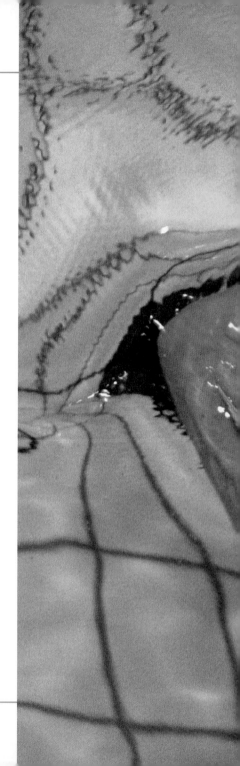

Backstroke moves a swimmer through the water at a **constant** speed. Swimmers doing the breaststroke push themselves through the water in a sudden burst. Then, they glide through the water. The breaststroke is three strokes in one: pull, then kick, then glide.

Swimmers start with their hands out ahead. They scoop down with both arms. Then they squeeze their arms together. This pushes the head out of the water so they can breathe. Then they dive forward into the water. They move their hands out ahead and kick with both feet. Then they glide through the water. When swimmers feel themselves slowing down, they take another stroke.

Streamline!

This stroke begins and ends in a **streamlined** position. Streamlined swimmers glide through the water smoothly. Swimmers put their feet together behind and their hands together in front of them. They pull their elbows tight against the ears.

Pull Practice

Here are some drills to help you with your stroke:

- **2 Pulls, 1 Kick:** This drill helps practice the breaststroke pull. Make a good pull (but don't kick) then glide. Then pull, kick, and glide normally. Repeat.

- **2 Kicks, 1 Pull:** This drill is the opposite of 2 Pulls, 1 Kick. It gives extra kick practice. First kick (without pulling), then glide. Then pull, kick, and glide.

- **Kick on Back:** Swimmers do the breaststroke kick lying on their back. Their hands are at their sides. They try not to let their knees break the surface. This helps practice keeping the knees below the waist during the kick.

- **Touch Your Heels:** Swimmers put their hands at their hips, a little behind their back. They kick across the pool. They try to touch their heels to their fingers between each kick.

No Frog Kicks!

Breaststroke swimmers should never spread their knees wide and kick like a frog. The knees should stay about shoulder-width apart. People's knees aren't built like a frog's knees. Frog kicks can lead to injury.

Float Like a Butterfly

Butterfly is the most tiring of the four strokes. It is also the hardest to learn. When done right , butterfly is fast and graceful.

Swimmers start with their hands in front. Then they pull the water down past their hips with both hands. As their hands come out of the water, they do a **dolphin kick**. This kick is done with the feet together. They pump their hips down, then up. At the same time, they pick their face up out of the water.

Next they swing their hands over the surface of the water. Their hands are now in front of them. They take a quick breath. Finally they dive their hands and face back into the water. Then they do another dolphin kick.

Are You Hip?

A dolphin kick uses the motion of the hips. Butterfly swimmers don't bend their knees. They let them stay flexible. The feet follow the hips through the water.

Try the Fly

The butterfly is a tough stroke. Here are some drills to help practice.

- **Dolphin Kick Practice:** The dolphin kick is the most important part of the butterfly. The key to this kick is moving the body up and down. The motion is like a dolphin leaping through the waves. Swimmers try to feel their body ripple through the water. They put their hands at their sides and feel the ripple move from their head to their hips to their feet. Next, they get into the streamlined position and feel the ripple again.

- **One-Arm Drills:** Swimmers do the butterfly with one side of their body at a time. They use a complete dolphin kick. Only one arm pulls through the water (kind of like swimming freestyle). They practice the rhythm of kicking and pulling. (A one-arm drill with a flutter kick is good for freestyle practice, too.)

Dive In!

Swimmers compete in races to see how fast they can go. A good race begins with a good start. Freestyle, breaststroke, and butterfly races begin when swimmers dive off platforms called **blocks**. Backstrokers can't dive backwards. They start in the water with special starts of their own.

Officials standing on the **deck** start the races. They blow whistles or shoot off cap guns. Racers start when they hear the noise.

Don't Start Too Soon

If a swimmer leaves the block too soon, it's called a false start. The official might start the race over. Swimmers who **false-start** can be *disqualified*. The race may be restarted without them. Practicing starts is important. A swimmer doesn't want to miss out on a race because he or she started too early.

Let's Get Started

Here's what to do when starting a race:

	Freestyle/ Breaststroke/Butterfly	Backstroke
1. "Swimmers, step up."	Swimmers stand on the blocks. Their toes curl over the edge.	Swimmers get in the water. They hold on to the backstroke bar on the front of the block. They put their toes just under water level.
2. "Take Your Marks."	They bend over at the hips. They grab the bottom of the block to steady themselves.	They pull in tight to the block.
3. BLAM!	They push on the block with their hands. This starts them moving forward. They spring up and out in a streamlined position.	They spring up and back. They tilt back their head. They throw their arms up and out.

Spin Me 'Round

One thing about all swimming pools is that they have walls. When swimmers reach a wall, they have to turn around. Most swimmers just touch the wall and push away. Racing swimmers do special turns so they can change directions very quickly.

Butterfly and breaststroke use an **open turn**. Swimmers touch the wall with both hands at the same time. The chest faces the bottom of the pool. They take a deep breath. Then they begin to swing around. They drop one shoulder into the water. Now they are on their side. They swing their feet under their body. Their toes are touching the wall. They reach their arms above their head. Now they are streamlined. Finally, they use their legs to spring off the wall and swim away.

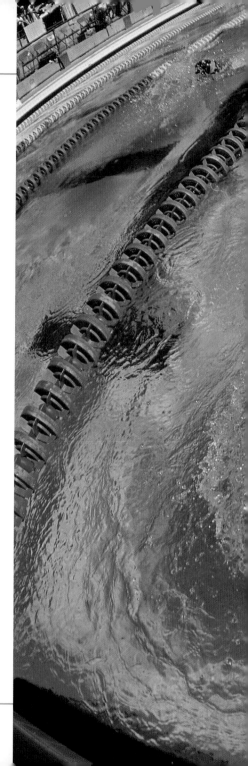

Freestyle and backstroke use a **flip turn**. This turn is a little harder, but it is very fast.

If swimmers are swimming backstroke, they roll over. They put their hands at their sides. Then, they duck their head toward the bottom. They tuck their chin to their chest. They throw their hands up past their face. The motion is like scooping water up over the shoulders. This starts them flipping! Their feet fly overhead and land against the wall. They streamline their arms. They push off with their feet.

How do swimmers know when to turn around? See page 6.

Putting It All Together

Once swimmers have learned all the strokes, they need to practice with their coach. Practicing happens in a workout. The coach plans what a swimmer will do. They will spend some time warming up. Then they'll get combinations of speeds, strokes, and distances called **sets**.

An important part of the set is its **intervals**. Intervals are how much time a swimmer has to swim a certain length of the pool. For instance, the coach might tell them to swim "five 25s on a 30." That means to swim twenty-five yards—one length of the pool—in thirty seconds. They have to do it five times.

A good workout is fun. It also gets a swimmer ready for races.

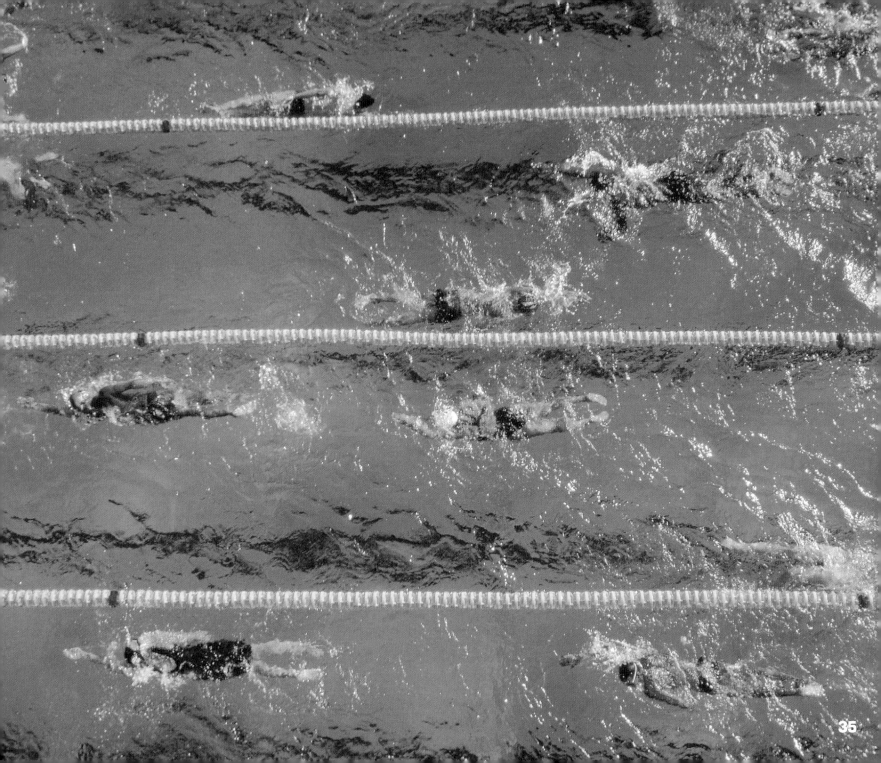

Off to the Races

A swimming competition is called a **meet**. A meet is a series of races, called **events**. Every event has its own stroke and distance. Each event at a meet is divided into **heats**. Each heat has one swimmer in each lane.

In some meets, the fastest swimmers from all the heats race against each other in a final heat. In other meets, swimmers only swim the race once. The winner of the event is the one with the fastest time.

Points are given to the teams of the top finishers in the event. The team with the most points at the end of the meet wins. For many swimmers, the most important part of the meet isn't whether they win. It's whether they swam faster than they had before.

Duke Paoa Kahanamoku (Lane #5) of the U.S. prepares to start a swimming event during the 1920 Olympic Games in Antwerp, Belgium.

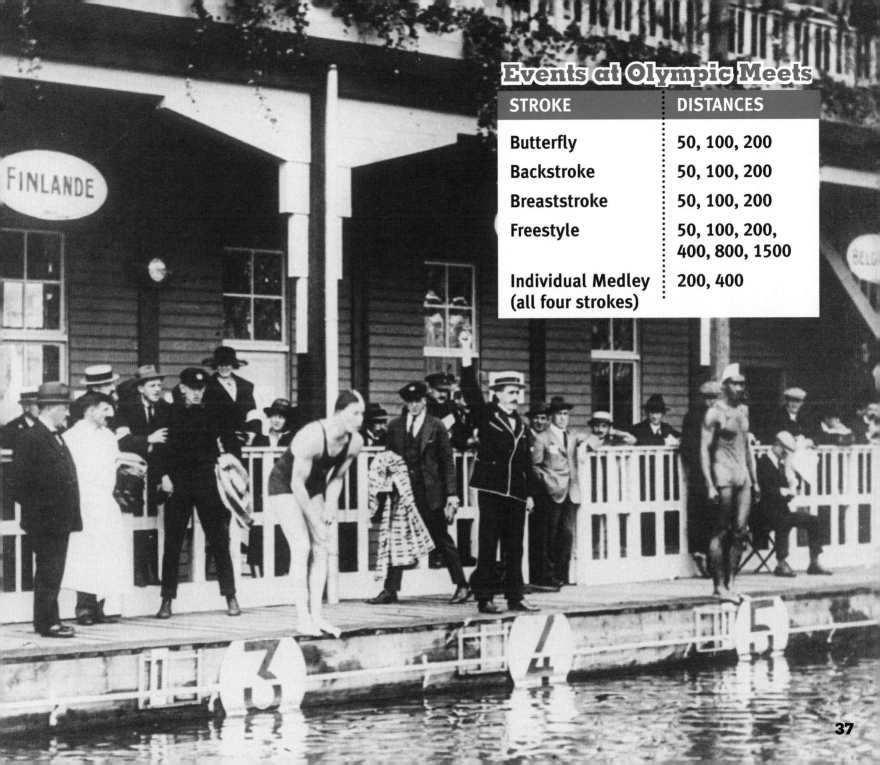

Events at Olympic Meets

STROKE	DISTANCES
Butterfly	50, 100, 200
Backstroke	50, 100, 200
Breaststroke	50, 100, 200
Freestyle	50, 100, 200, 400, 800, 1500
Individual Medley (all four strokes)	200, 400

FINLANDE

Team Efforts

Most races at meets are individual events. Swimmers get in and race against everyone else in the pool. **_Relay_** races use teams. Four swimmers work together to win a race for their team.

In a relay, each team member swims the same distance. When one swimmer finishes a **_leg_** of the race, one of his or her teammates dives off the blocks. The first team to go through all four swimmers wins. Relays are a fun and exciting part of any meet or practice.

Be Careful!

Make sure not to leave early. If a swimmer dives in before his or her teammate touches the wall, the team is disqualified. Relay swimmers practice starts so they can time their dives correctly.

Fish In the Water

Janet Evans and Mark Spitz are famous even among the swimming greats.

Janet Evans

Janet Evans is called the "Queen of the Distance Swimmers." She was born on August 28, 1971. She grew up in Placentia, California. Evans set her first U.S. record at age ten. Evans dominated long-distance events: the 400, 800, and 1500 freestyle, and the 400 individual medley. During her career, she won forty-five U.S. National Championships, competed in three Olympics, won five Olympic medals, and set seven world records.

Mark Spitz

Mark Spitz is amazing! He was born February 10, 1950. He grew up in Modesto, California. Spitz held seventeen national titles by the age of ten. He won four medals at the 1968 Olympics in Mexico City. At the 1972 Olympics, he won an amazing seven gold medals! He won the 100 and 200 freestyle and butterfly events plus three relays. He set world records in every one of them!

What Happened When?

9000 B.C.	2000 B.C.	0 A.D.	1500	1600	1870	1880

9000 B.C. Paintings of swimmers are made on cave walls in Libya.

2100 B.C. Egyptian nobles teach their children to swim.

100 B.C. The first use of a special bathing costume is recorded in Greece.

36 B.C. Swim races are recorded in Japan.

1448 Swimming is mentioned in records of Inca people.

1538 *Art of Swimming* is published in Europe.

1603 Swimming becomes part of basic education in Japan.

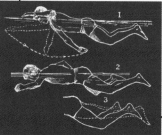

1873 Arthur Trudgen brings a freestyle arm stroke to Europe after seeing it in South America. Europeans use it with a breaststroke kick and call it the "Trudgen" stroke.

1875 The first English Channel swim is completed by Capt. Matthew Webb. It is not repeated until 1911.

1883 The first U.S. national meet is held.

1890　1900　1910　1920　1930　1950　1960　1970　1980　1990　2000

1896 First modern Olympics features four men's swimming events, all freestyle.

1900 Backstroke is added to Olympics.

1902 Richard Cavill teaches modern freestyle stroke, learned from South Pacific Islanders, in England. It uses a flutter kick.

1904 First Olympic breaststroke races are held.

1908 Féderation Internationale de Natation Amateur (FINA) is founded—the first international swimming organization.

1912 First women's Olympic swimming events are held.

1926 Gertrude Ederle becomes first woman to swim English Channel, and sets new speed record while doing it.

1952 Previously considered a version of breaststroke, butterfly becomes an official stroke in international competition.

1964 Fourteen-year-old Lillian "Pokey" Watson becomes the youngest American to win an Olympic swimming medal.

1973 The first World Swimming Championships (aside from Olympics) are held by FINA.

1988 Anthony Nesty of Suriname, a tiny South American country with only one Olympic-sized pool, wins a gold medal at the Seoul Olympics.

2000 Jenny Thompson wins her tenth Olympic medal, a record for American women.

Super Swimming Facts

In the Middle Ages, Europeans stayed out of the water as much as they could. They thought it caused disease. Now we put chemicals such as chlorine into pools to keep them clean.

Until the 1930s, most bathing suits covered the body from neck to knee. They were made of cotton or wool. They were very heavy when wet!

People keep backyard pools warm for splashing around. Hard exercise in warm water is tiring. Workout pools are kept at about 79°F (26°C).

John V. Sigmund made the longest nonstop swim ever in 1940. He swam 292 miles (470 kilometers) of the Mississippi River in eighty-nine hours and forty-two minutes.

The most famous open-water swim isn't a race. It's swimming across the English Channel, from England to France! This twenty-one-mile (thirty-four-kilometer) journey has been made by nearly six hundred people since 1875.

England
English—
Channel
France

► The youngest person was Thomas Gregory, age eleven years eleven months, in 1988.

► Alison Streeter has done it the most—forty times!

► Philip Rush swam from England to France to England to France—three crossings—in twenty-eight hours twenty-one minutes!

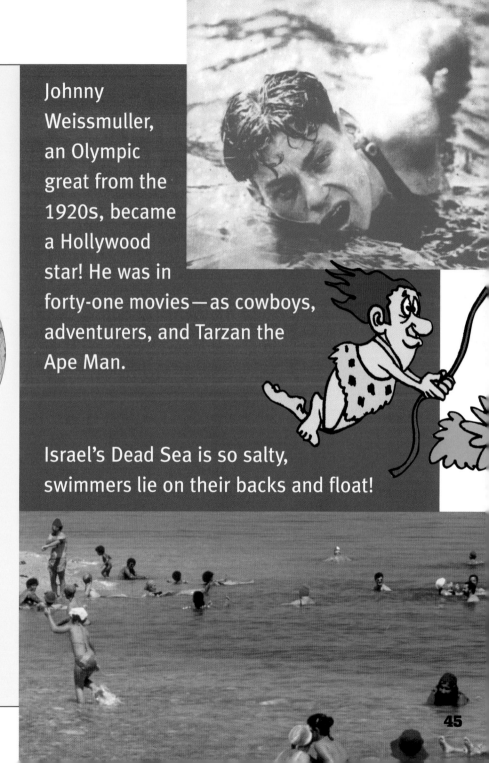

Johnny Weissmuller, an Olympic great from the 1920s, became a Hollywood star! He was in forty-one movies—as cowboys, adventurers, and Tarzan the Ape Man.

Israel's Dead Sea is so salty, swimmers lie on their backs and float!

Swimming Words to Know

backstroke: stroke swum on your back, with a flutter kick and alternating arm strokes. Called "back" for short.

backstroke flags: rope of colorful plastic flags hung over pool near each end, warning backstrokers that they are approaching the wall

blocks: starting platforms at one end (or both ends) of each lane

bottom lines: dark lines at the bottom of the pool that mark the center of each lane

breaststroke: front stroke swum using unique knee-bending kick and short, scooping arm motions. Called "breast" for short.

butterfly: front stroke where swimmer pulls with both arms at once and uses a dolphin kick. Called "fly" for short.

dolphin kick: unique kick where swimmer keeps feet together and makes up-and-down hip motions

deck: walkway surrounding pool

drag: resistance of the water against a swimmer's body or swim equipment. Drag slows swimmers down.

false start: in a race, leaving the blocks too early. A false start is grounds for disqualification.

flip turn: somersaulting turn used by freestyle and backstroke swimmers

flutter kick: kick using alternating left and right legs in up-and-down motions

freestyle: front stroke using a flutter kick and alternating arm strokes. Called "free" for short.

gutter: trough surrounding pool that contains and dampens turbulence

individual medley (IM): event featuring equal parts butterfly, backstroke, breaststroke, and freestyle, swum in that order and without stopping

interval: amount of time given to swimmers during a workout to travel a specific distance

lane lines: cables strung across pool to separate pool into lanes and to dampen turbulence

long-course: a pool 50 meters or yards in length; or a race held in a 50-meter or 50-yard pool. See also short-course.

open turn: two-handed turn used by butterfly and breaststroke swimmers, also called a touch turn

open-water: a race held in a body of water that isn't a pool, such as in a river, lake, or ocean

recovery: bringing the arm from the ending position to the starting position in a stroke, usually done above the water

rotation: a side-to-side rocking motion that is a key component of freestyle and backstroke

set: a combination of distances, strokes, and intervals assigned to swimmers during a workout

short-course: a pool 25 meters or yards in length; or a race held in a 25-meter or 25-yard pool. See also long-course.

streamlined: body position creating as little drag as possible; feet together, legs straight, arms above head, hands together, elbows tight against ears

T: T-shaped mark at either end of the bottom line, warning swimmers that they are approaching the wall

target: cross-shaped mark in the middle of the wall at both ends of each lane; helps swimmers swim in straight lines and turn smoothly

Metric Conversion
1 foot = .3048 meters
1 yard = .9144 meters

Other Words to Know

Here are definitions of some of the words used in this book:

consecutive: in a row, without stopping

constant: the same, without changing

dampen: to decrease

disqualify: to remove from a race or contest due to rule breakage

event: a single race or contest during a larger sporting event

heat: a single trial of a small group of athletes at a time during a sporting event

injuries: parts of the body that are hurt, which can happen when playing sports

leg: in a relay race, the portion of the race done by any single member of the relay team

meet: sporting event featuring many races or contests

relay: race in which members of a team each complete an equal portion of a larger distance

strategy: a plan or method to do something

turbulence: choppiness or rough motion of water

Where To Learn More

AT THE LIBRARY

Carter, Kyle. *Safety In Water.* Vero Beach, Fla.: Rourke Publishing, LLC, 1994.

Ditchfield, Christin. *Swimming and Diving.* New York: Scholastic Library Publishing, 2000.

Rouse, Jeff and James Jackson. *The Young Swimmer.* New York: DK Publishing, Inc., 1997.

ON THE ROAD

International Swimming Hall of Fame
One Hall of Fame Drive
Fort Lauderdale, FL 33316
954/462-6536
www.ishof.org

ON THE WEB

For more information on Swimming, use FactHound to track down Web sites related to this book.

1. Go to
www.compasspointbooks.com/facthound
2. Type in this book ID: 0756504325
3. Click on the *FETCH IT* button.

Your trusty FactHound will fetch the best Web sites for you!

INDEX

ABOUT THE AUTHOR
Andrew Willett grew up in the San Francisco Bay Area, where there's a swimming pool in nearly every backyard. Now he lives in New York City and is an enthusiastic Masters swimmer and coach with Team New York Aquatics. He has written and edited kids' books, trading cards, comic books, textbooks, pop-up ads, and educational games.